Outside the Box

Paul Holmes

On the Rhetoric of the Face: *Outside the Box*, by Paul Holmes - Louise S. Milne

Installation Photography - Alkistis Terzi

The Artist in Conversation with Rory MacLean

Additional Text - Haftor Medbøe

www.paul-holmes.org

Cover illustration: Waveform details from the four unheard music tracks played in the course of the work.

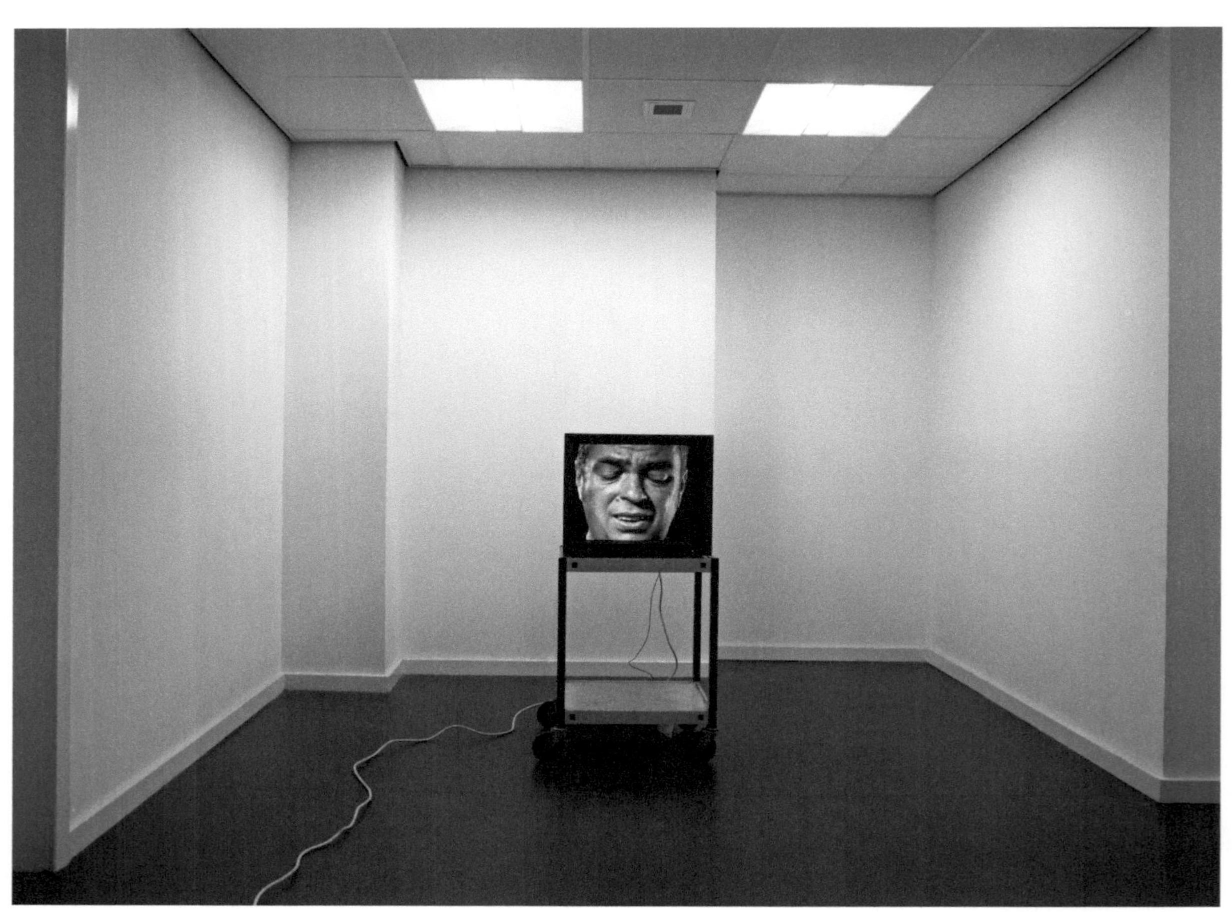

Outside the Box

In the summer of 2013 I went to see The Haftor Medbøe Group at the Edinburgh Jazz and Blues Festival. The music was everything we have come to expect of contemporary jazz: original, uplifting, energetic, dangerous. The musicianship was scintillating, yet my gaze was increasingly distracted from the work the players were doing with their hands and their instruments, and drawn instead to the gurnings and contortions their faces were making as they played.

As the group improvised their way through a unique and never-to-be-repeated piece of music, these involuntary expressions seemed to me to embody the creative process in its rawest state, with its associated jeopardies and elations, agonies and triumphs.

I had already begun exploring the power of the face as the subject for moving image work in my video piece *Time Machine* and these musicians' extraordinary facial ticks and tells presented an opportunity to explore this preoccupation on a larger scale and in a more ambitious project.

The work shows the faces of the band-members as they rehearse their way through a four-track set, divorced from any spatial or geographical context; in complete silence; at one remove from each other; and with no visual sense of the instruments they are playing. The piece is in black and white and screens on a 4:3 traditional 'cube' style CRT monitor installed on the gallery floor. The inference for the viewer is that these bobbing, suffering faces are trapped in an electronic box.

I had known Rory MacLean for some time and we had often spoken about collaborating on a research project that explored the psychology of creativity. It quickly became clear to me that the raw footage and the soundtrack we recorded as by-products to the production of the artwork would provide an exciting platform to examine the creative work being done by the musicians on a moment-by-moment basis. Now the artwork is complete we can begin the research in earnest. Our initial conversations, after having watched the footage, are documented here.

Louise Milne and I have been teaching colleagues for many years. I was delighted when she agreed to write an essay about the work. She is someone I admire greatly as a critic and practitioner and her lucid prose helps to uncover the meaning of the work in a way that is both refreshing and exhilarating.

I am grateful to Edinburgh Napier University for funding the project; to the University of the West of Scotland where I developed so much of my new work; to the production team; to Alkistis Terzi and her camera crew for the work's luminous black and white cinematography; to Haftor Medbøe and his band: Espen Eriksen, Dave Kane and Andrew Lisle; and to Sean Martin for his patience and hard work putting together the book.

This book is being published to coincide with my solo exhibition *Outside the Box* at Studio 21 gallery in Kolkata, India. I'd like to acknowledge the support the Indian Council for Cultural Relations and the British Council in Kolkata gave me while in India. I'd also like to thank the Scottish Centre for Tagore Studies and Rabindra Bharati University for sending me to Kolkata in the first place. Most of all, my grateful thanks to the Studio 21's curator, Manas Acharya, for giving me the opportunity to show my work in that great city.

Paul Holmes, June 2015

Individualisation is cherished in this music and the outcome a collective tapestry of interpretation and approach. The aim is to transcend both the limits of the composer's imagination and the physical demands of instrumental performance in creating a moment in time that is greater than the sum of its parts.

On the Rhetoric of the Face: *Outside the Box*, by Paul Holmes

Louise S. Milne

The box frames a head, alive, intent, grimacing, rocking slightly. Watch awhile and this head is replaced by another, and another – four in all – each face caught in a paroxysm of rhythmic movement, eyes fixed on some object beyond our view. They are all male, three in late youth, one older. And there is no sound. Just the faces in the box, moving. What are they doing? *Outside the Box* presents the viewer with something that announces itself as a puzzle. The monochrome, the silence, the framing of these agitated heads initiate a sense of abstraction. Since the context which (we assume) would enable us to understand the scenario is withheld, we are compelled to supply it from the cultural field. A complex skein of traditions and conventions about the face in visual representation comes into play, to do with portraiture, physiognomy, and the nature of expression.

In the first age of illusionistic art, Leonardo wrote that the goal of portraiture was to show the movements of the mind.[4] His own paintings and drawings, based on studies of anatomy and expression, demonstrate how this was to be done: the artist must exaggerate, to a greater or lesser extent, the muscles under the skin, making them visible on the surface of the face and body. The resulting visual pattern - of lines, light and shadow - is read as the signature of an internal, animating force; the mind (*anima*) operating the face. It is easier

TIME IS. TIME WAS. TIME'S PAST.
Words spoken by the magic head of brass, created by Roger Bacon[1]

The riddle conceals what wit reveals... in riddles, the manner is known, and the matter [is] to be discovered.
Ernst Kris (1952)[2]

There is no close-up of the face. The close-up is the face... a nudity of the face is much greater than that of the body... the single and ravaged face...
Gilles Deleuze (1983)[3]

The analysis [of] gesture into its incremental displacements... creating minute variations... jerked into motion by their passage through the camera's gate... all this [is] a resource of the beat...
Rosalind Krauss (1988)[5]

produce this effect for an aged face, which already bears the marks of its muscles on its skin, than for a young one; this is why the older face of the quartet in *Outside the Box* appears more compelling, more magnetic.

After Leonardo, artists such as Bernini developed his techniques to construct faces intended to convey religious passion or ecstasy, as propaganda for the counter-reformation.[6] Charles Lebrun (1619-90), Louis XIV's court painter, tried to systematize the whole issue of facial expression (figs. 1a, 1b). In a famous lecture to the newly constituted Académie Royale de Peinture et de Sculpture in 1668,[7] later published, he presented drawings of faces exhibiting specific emotions (admiration, fear etc), plus analyses of why this should be the case. Lebrun drew freely on classical and modern theories of mind to back up his system; he argued, for example, that the key importance of eyebrows in facial expression was due to their proximity to the brain, the seat of the soul.[8]

Though Lebrun was wrong about this (and much else), the pseudo-science of physiognomy which he founded (along with its shady cousin, phrenology[9]) enjoyed huge success. Whether or not people in real life had ever previously distorted their faces to convey emotion in the ways Lebrun described, by the era of photography (1839) and early cinema (c. 1898) we can see that they certainly were doing so; generations of writers, artists and actors took their repertoire of expression from Lebrun and his successors. This rhetoric of the face entered the vocabulary of popular performance, where it continues to flourish.

Tell me where is Fancie bred / ...in the heart or in the head? / How begot, how nourished? / Replie, replie! / It is engendered in the eyes / With gazing fed... / Ding, dong, bell / Ding, dong, bell
The Merchant of Venice
III.2.64-70

The emotions always have a quite definite class basis; the form they take at any time is historical, restricted and limited in specific ways. The emotions are in no sense universally human and timeless.
Bertolt Brecht (1940)[10]

Fig. 1a. After Charles Lebrun, *Attention*, 1740-65. Engraving, 27.8x18.8cm. British Museum 1925,0417.1.2.

Fig. 1b. After Charles Lebrun, *Acute Pain*, 1740-65. Engraving, 28.1x18.4cm. British Museum 1925,0417.1.10.

Fig. 2. Messerschmidt heads exhibited at Louvre Museum, Paris, part of the exhibition *Franz Xaver Messerschmidt (1736 – 1783)*; photo: O. Benton (2015), after MKP-0508 (2011).

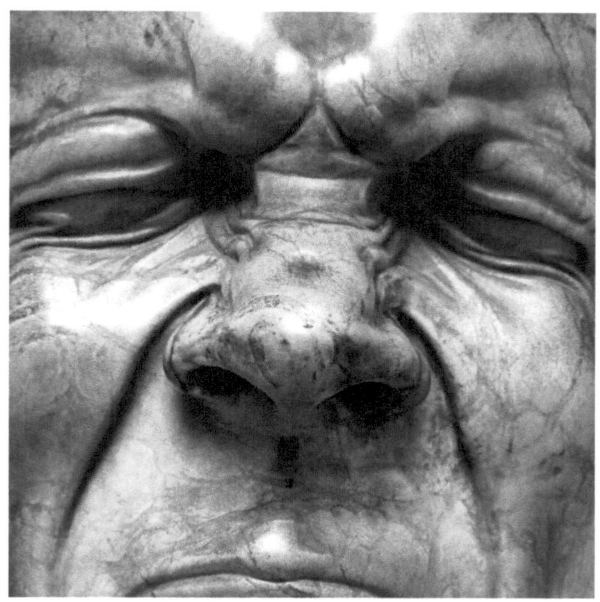

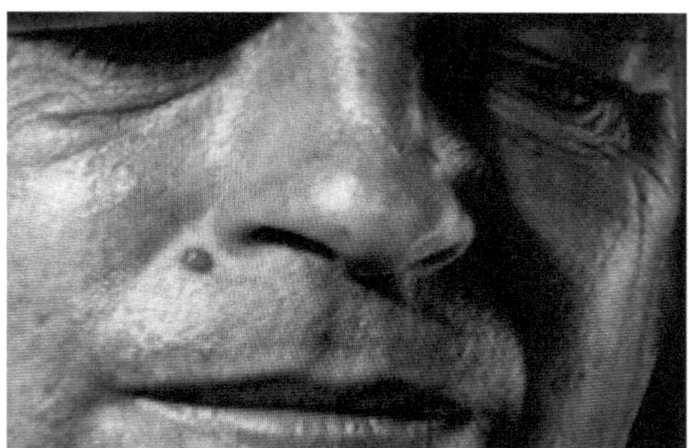

Fig. 3. Franz Xaver Messerschmidt, *The Vexed Man*, 1771-83. Alabaster, 39.4x27.3x 26cm. The J. Paul Getty Museum 2008.4.

Fig. 4. Paul Holmes, still, featuring Haftor Medbøe, from *Outside the Box*, 2015.

Lebrun's views were part of a wider shift in Western thought and taste. The Enlightenment is often remembered as a triumph of logic and rationality. It is more accurate rather to see it as a search for transparency in all things. The central aesthetic category in 18C art, literature and philosophy was *sensibilité*:[11] overwhelming sentiment, ideally felt and transmitted as directly as possible, and, of course, therefore directly visible on the face.

The German sculptor Franz Xaver Messerschmidt (1736-83; figs. 2 and 3) spent much of his life working on a series of "character studies"[13] – based on his own head – depicting extremes of physiognomy. And here is where the rhetoric of the face takes a darker turn. In fact, despite the apparent super-legibility of Messerschmidt's heads, it is by no means clear what each expression is supposed to signify.[14] Like the "hysterics" photographed so assiduously by the early French pioneer psychiatrist Jean-Martin Charcot (1825-93), what is written on these faces remains unreadable. Charcot was "un visuel," wrote Freud, his student, "not a thinker, not an intellectual,"[16] and what he visualised in the faces of his leading ladies was the constructed phenomenon of hysteria, a catch-all diagnosis for mental disturbance. Charcot's photographs were used most tellingly by André Breton and Louis Aragon, who published them in the Surrealist journal in 1929 as an exemplar of the mysteries of the mind, rather than its transparencies.[17]

I have arrived at the point where the movement of my thought interests me more than my thought itself.
Pablo Picasso (c. 1963)[12]

the grandness / of my head / boned / tower of thought / tough coconut.../ protecting / the clockworks... / guarding / treasures infinitesimal / arteries, incredible / circulations / pulses of reason.../ ...and in them / will, the fish of movement / the electric corolla / of stimulus...
Pablo Neruda (1957)[15]

As image-makers developed the lens-based media, they
further problematised the certainties inherited from
Lebrun et al. In Moscow in 1923, Lev Kuleshov (1899-1970)
conducted his seminal experiments in film editing,
demonstrating that the same shot of an actor's face could
be plausibly used to convey a character's reactions to a)
being given a bowl of soup and b) being released from
prison.[18] Kuleshov and his circle called for a new style of
film acting, rejecting the "psychological-theatrical"
mode, derived from live drama, that then held sway.[19]
Mastery of montage enabled the modernist avant-garde to
reject the inherited weight of *sensibilité* in its 19C
codified form; the rest of the 20C followed suit. The
iconic film stars of the postwar period exhibited "cool"
or deadpan performance styles; Rudolf Valentino gave way
to Robert Mitchum.

In 1970, the American artist Douglas Huebler (1924-
97) designed and conducted *Duration Piece #14*.[21] Keeping
constant as many parameters as possible (time of day,
clothing, pose, venue), he asked a group of participants
to think of the emotion or object he showed them on a
flash card, then he photographed them as they were doing
this. Pairs of words were used on each successive day
(love/war, monster/kitten etc). The resulting photos,
along with the explanatory text, form the piece. The
photos, naturally, are indistinguishable from each other.
Here we have the origin of the puzzle presented in
Holmes's piece: the face as a visual riddle.

Huebler's work terminates another strand of the
sensibilité tradition; for him – as for Kuleshov – the
movements of the mind need have no visible trace in facial
expression at all; only context – that is, external
information – allows us to interpret depicted faces. The
Messerschmidt and Huebler styles of expression present,
then, two ends of the spectrum in the Western rhetoric of
the face – contorted versus blank – making it clear that

Whenever Mitchum is on camera
or on tape, in character or
in person... he always seems to
be declaring the primacy of
things we do not know about
him... what [he does] is not
really acting at all; it is
more like performing...
physically convincing us that
the actions we see arise from
a coherent source to which we
have no access, and cannot
understand.
Dave Hickey (1997)[20]

I have that within which
passeth show...
Hamlet 1.2.85

all we can securely read in this rhetoric is emotional
excitation, or the lack of it. These two poles correspond
to Lacanian distinction between *excess* and *deficit* of
affect (emotion). As visual signs, one type is overloaded,
the other underwhelmed; one is climactic, the other
static. Deleuze argued that, in the grammar of cinema, the
close-up of the face is the ultimate signifier of *affect*,[22]
from its foundation devised as a tool to communicate
emotion. It has three formal means of achieving this: the
tight frame on the performer's head, inducing empathy in
the viewer and the expectation of empathetic meaning; the
facial expression supplied by the performer (extreme,
deadpan, or somewhere in between); and the Kuleshovian
syntax effected by the shots on either side.

    On the smaller screen of television, and in
documentary, the close-up of the face is deployed more
extensively, not just for reaction shots, but as the
dominant format: television is the medium of the talking
head. Artists such as Bruce Nauman, Barbara Kruger and
Gillian Wearing, using video in an antagonistic or avant-
garde relation to mainstream culture, thus deploy the
close-up as a convention – denoting political or news
broadcasts, TV interviews and *vox pop* – in order to
subvert it. Thus Nauman presented the shaven head of the
singer Rinde Eckert, revolving and intoning, on three
giant screens (some upside down) and six monitors; Kruger
recorded actors delivering hate-speeches, simultaneously
and in sequence, on multiple monitors; Wearing shuffled
faces and speeches, to make a work where adults voiced the
thoughts and gestures of children.[25]

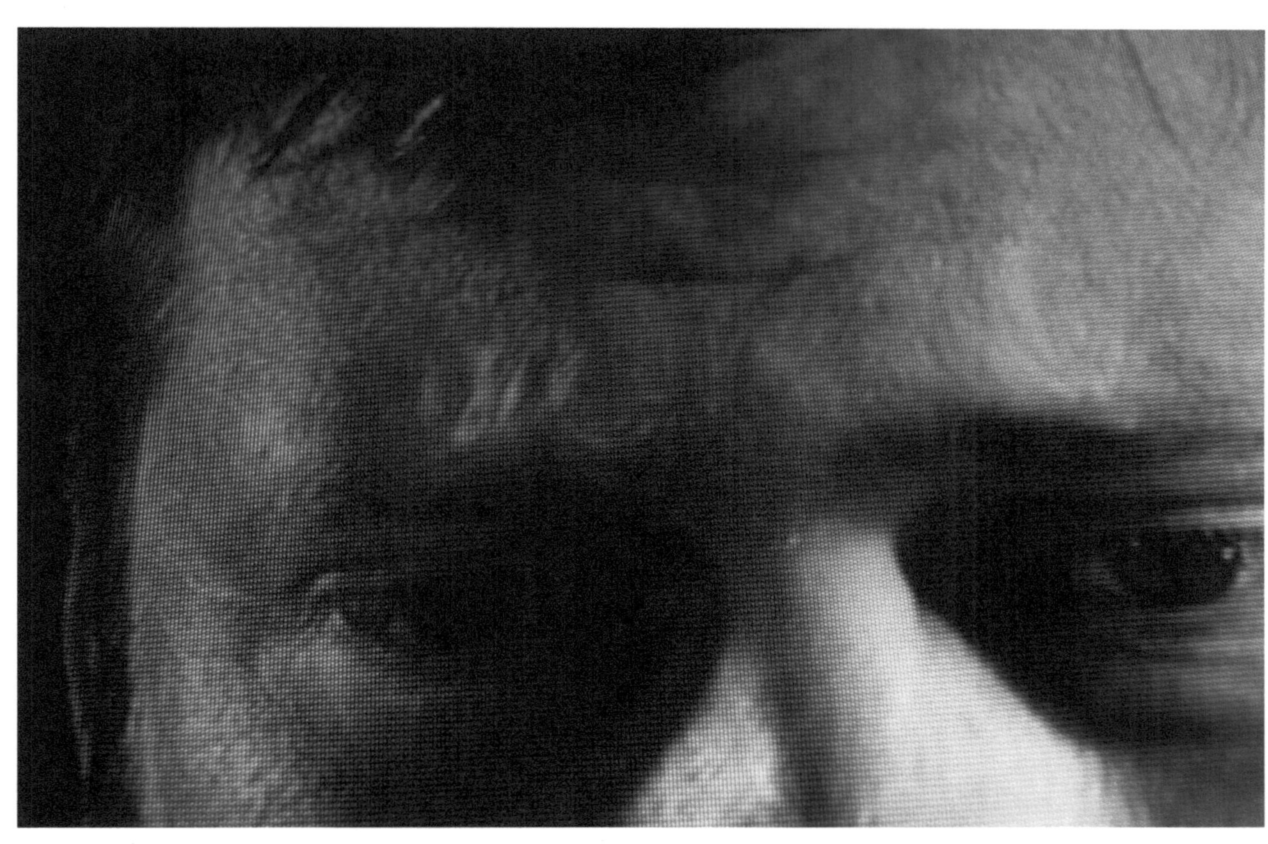

The improviser often takes the narrative into uncharted territories, if only to force an untested resolution to a problem of its own making. Mistakes are, in this sense, welcomed as events that elicit immediate reaction and response — calling on the problem-solving skill base of musical experience.

In these and similar works, faces in close-up are internally contextualised, through the use of multiple screens, text, and especially sound: in art video, the close-up is part of the discourse of the *talking* head. Georgina Starr, and more recently Bill Viola, have created video work showing people crying, or apparently in the grip of strong emotion. Viola's *Dolorosa* and *Six Heads* (2000), for example, in his ongoing *Passions* series, present formal parallels to Holmes's silent faces. The *Six Heads*, shorn of their necks and photoshopped together on a black background, exhibit a Messerschmidt-like series of exaggerated expressions. Costume, context and framing are designed to link these excruciated performers to the Christian tradition. Viola clearly hopes that his dramatised enactments of intense emotion, coupled with the iconographic cues he supplies, will convey spiritual, as opposed to secular passion.

But, as with Messerschmidt's heads, or Kuleshov's actor, on their own, the facial expressions cannot secure linkage with a desired brand of emotion, and so resist the tragic tone Viola intends. Bear in mind that Huebler did not ask his people to *act out* feelings of love/hate etc – that would immediately have brought into play the bathetic cultural package set up by Lebrun et al (something of the kind that is happening in the Violas). Which returns us to the issue of *performed* expression and its codification in culture. The heads of *Outside the Box*, though silent, are clearly in action. Their movement strongly suggests carnal excitation of some sort, because it expresses a rhythm. And rhythm, visible in a moving head, in a television, requires us to see it as performance.

Holmes's tightly framed faces, in Deleuzian terms, represent a text book case of the close-up as cinematic affect; Holmes has also constructed this piece as a kind of test or investigation of the theory. The choice of monochrome both acts as a reference to classic cinema, and

intensifies the Lebrun/Messerschmidt effect of graphic
expression. As a shot sequence, by Kuleshov's rules, the
four faces contextualise each other. We are compelled to
read the heads, and their expressions, as bound together.
The quotidian dimension of the photographic image – we see
their pores, their sweat – works to reinforce the
mesmerising impact, and also to produce a voyeuristic
comic effect. Their rhythmic rocking is perceived as the
symptom of a *shared* stimulus: a somatic pulse, located
beyond the frame. This pulse, running in series through
the shots of all four heads, operates in tandem with the
faces like a carrying wave, whose bursts of signal are the
periodic excruciated clenches of grimace, never
terminating in stillness.

Lyotard wrote of this pulse as a phenomenon of the
matrix, the interface between conscious and unconscious:
the on/off of embodied desire. As Krauss pointed out, part
of the affect of this phantasmic pulse is the fear that it
will be interrupted. So the anxiety/fear/anticipation of
the end of desire is itself wound in to desire: the fear
that the ego will cease, along with its carrying wave,
shattering in catharsis (climax) or decomposing in death.
All performance is pulse-based in this sense. Its object
is to convey the carrying wave of excitation – a rhythm –
which the performer must maintain, simultaneously
navigating and generating its climactic patterns without
becoming actually overwhelmed. The performer's goal is to
appear to be immersed in the action of performance – more
precisely, to give the impression of being *in danger* of
losing the self completely – without, of course, doing so.
This is the case in shamanic performance, the point of
which is to convince the audience – not necessarily the
shaman – that a spirit journey is taking place.[33] Notice
that this is the case whether or not any kind of self-loss
is in fact being experienced by the performer; we are
concerned here with the rhetoric of the face in visual

representation, not the internal experience. *Outside the Box* invites us to recognise both our lack of access to that internal experience, and our conviction that it exists, by isolating the codes of the rhetoric which mediates between the two.

As an aspect of style – as a code of expression – the enactment of self-loss mediates between excess and deficit. In the modern West, from around 1900, this performance mode arose originally in counter-cultural practices of dance and music, where participants and performers alike sought relief from self in somatic experience, to gain release of, and from, the tensions and repressions of working life. Subsequently, as counter-cultural genres spread into mainstream popular culture – in particular, as they entered the visual mass media – the mode of self-loss was adopted both as a hallmark of authenticity and as a means of encouraging empathy and identification from the audience – exactly as the close-up does in the Deleuzian reading of cinema.

Thus we read the ingredients of *Outside the Box* – the close-up frame, the facial extremes, the rocking, rhythm and monochrome – not simply as expressive of affect but as commentary on the media of affect. And here the Kuleshovian aspect is crucial, for we must also take Holmes's heads in relation to each other. Unlike Lebrun's "transparent" expressions, or Messerschmidt's paroxysms, they do not form a series but a sequence. Leonardo's "movements of the mind" becomes rather a movement between minds, whose constant is rhythm, a pulse of managed desire. Whatever they are doing, they do it together, on the beat.

Notes

1. Anon., "The Head of Brass," in Amabel William-Ellis, *Fairy Tales from the British Isles* (London, 1966), 186-95.

2. Ernst Kris, "A Psychotic Sculptor of the Eighteenth Century" (1952), in his *Psychoanalytic Explorations in Art* (New York, 1974), 176.

3. Gilles Deleuze, *Cinema 1* (1983), trans. Hugh Tomlinson & Barbara Habberjam (London, 2005), 102.

4. MS. 2038 Bib. Nat. 19r & v, 20r.; *The Notebooks of Leonardo da Vinci*, ed., trans. and Intro. Edward MacCurdy (New York, 1939), 854.

5. Rosalind Krauss, "The Im/pulse to See," in H. Foster, ed., *Vision and Visuality*, Discussions in Contemporary Culture no. 2 (Seattle, 1988), 67.

6. The word *propaganda* is here used in its original sense: "Congregation or College of the Propaganda... A committee of Cardinals of the Roman Catholic Church having the care and over-sight of foreign missions, founded in 1622 by Pope Gregory XV," *Oxford English Dictionary*.

7. Later published by attendee Henri Testelin in *Sentiments des plus habiles peintres sur la pratique de la peinture et de la sculpture mis en tables de préceptes* (Paris, 1680; 1696); L. Cottegnies, "Codifying the Passions in the Classical Age: a few reflections on Charles Le Brun's scheme and its influence in France and England," *Etudes Epistémè*, 1 (2002), 141.

8. Cottegnies, 143-4.

9. Phrenology, hugely popular in the 19C, was the practice of interpreting bumps on the head as signs of character.

10. Bertolt Brecht, "Short Description of a New Technique of Acting," in J. Willett, ed. and trans., *Brecht on Theatre: The Development of an Aesthetic* (London, 1964), 145.

11. Norman Bryson, *Word and Image: French Painting of the Ancien Régime* (Cambridge, 1981), chs. 1, 4, 5.

12. Quoted in Françoise Gilot and Carlton Lake, *Life With Picasso* (1964; London, 1990), 124. Gilot lived with Picasso between 1953 and 1973.

13. Kris, 128-50; see Maria Pötzl-Malikova, 'The Life and Work of Franz Xaver Messerschmidt,' in Guilhem Scherf, Maria Pötzl-Malikova, eds., *Franz Xaver Messerschmidt 1736-1783: From Neoclassicism to Expressionism* (Paris-New York, 2010), 21-9, esp. 28 n.24 on Kris's theories and their later reception.

14. The current titles usually affixed to Messerschmidt's busts were attached ten years after the artist's death and are not accepted as accurate; Pötzl-Malikova, 23.

15. Pablo Neruda, *Ode to the Cranium (Oda al Cráneo)*, in his *Elemental Odes*, trans. Margaret Sayers Peden (London, 1994), 179-83.

16. Sigmund Freud, *Charcot* (1893), in James Strachey, ed. & trans., *Standard Edition of the Complete Psychological Works of Sigmund Freud*, III (London, 1962), 11-23.

17. "Le Cinquantenaire de l'hystérie," *La Révolution surréaliste* 11 (1928), 20-2.

18. Jay Leyda, *Kino: A History of the Russian and Soviet Film* (3rd ed.; Princeton, 1983), 165; Lev Kuleshov, "*Art of the Cinema* (1929)," in R. Levaco, ed., trans. & intro., *Kuleshov on Film: Writings* (University of California, 1974), 41-123.

19. Leyda, 172.

20. Dave Hickey, "Mitchum Gets Out of Jail," in L. Sante, M. H. Pierson, eds., *O.K. You Mugs: Writers on Movie Actors* (London, 2000), 14-5.

21. The Huebler work is illustrated in Lucy Lippard, *Six Years: The Dematerialization of the Art Object from 1966 to 1972* (1973), 120.

22. Deleuze goes on to argue that all close-ups of anything are in some sense turned into faces.

23. Deleuze, 89.

24. Stephen Heath, "Representing Television," in Patricia Mellencamp, ed., *Logics of Television: Essays in Cultural Criticism* (Indiana, 1990), 285.

25. The works I am thinking of here are: Bruce Nauman, *Anthro/Socio (Rinde Spinning)* (1991; 2015); Barbara Kruger, *Twelve* (2004) and *The Globe Shrinks* (2010); Gillian Wearing, *10-16* (1997).

26. Ernst Bloch, *Das Prinzip Hoffnung* (1960), 339; *The Principle of Hope* I, trans. Basil Blackwell (Michigan, 1995), 339.

27. Maurice Blanchot, *L'Entretien infini* (Paris, 1969), 364; "Everyday Speech," trans. Susan Hanson, *Yale French Studies* 73 (1987), 18-9.

28. Krauss, 67.

29. Deleuze, 91.

30. Christina Rossetti, *Goblin Market* (1862).

31. Krauss, 67.

32. Ornette Coleman in conversation (1995); David Toop, *Exotica: Fabricated Soundscapes in a Real World* (London, 1999), 185.

33. "The magnetism of shamanism [is] a strand in pop religion [and] an aesthetic that has stimulated such avant-garde artists and cultural radicals as Joseph Beuys... this type, with its transgressive capacities... [is] an exotic essence, a romanticized inversion of Western rationalism" Caroline Humphreys, "Introduction," in Nicholas Thomas & Caroline Humphrey, eds., *Shamanism, History and the State* (Michigan, 1994), 2.

34. Kris, 177.

35. Krauss, 68.

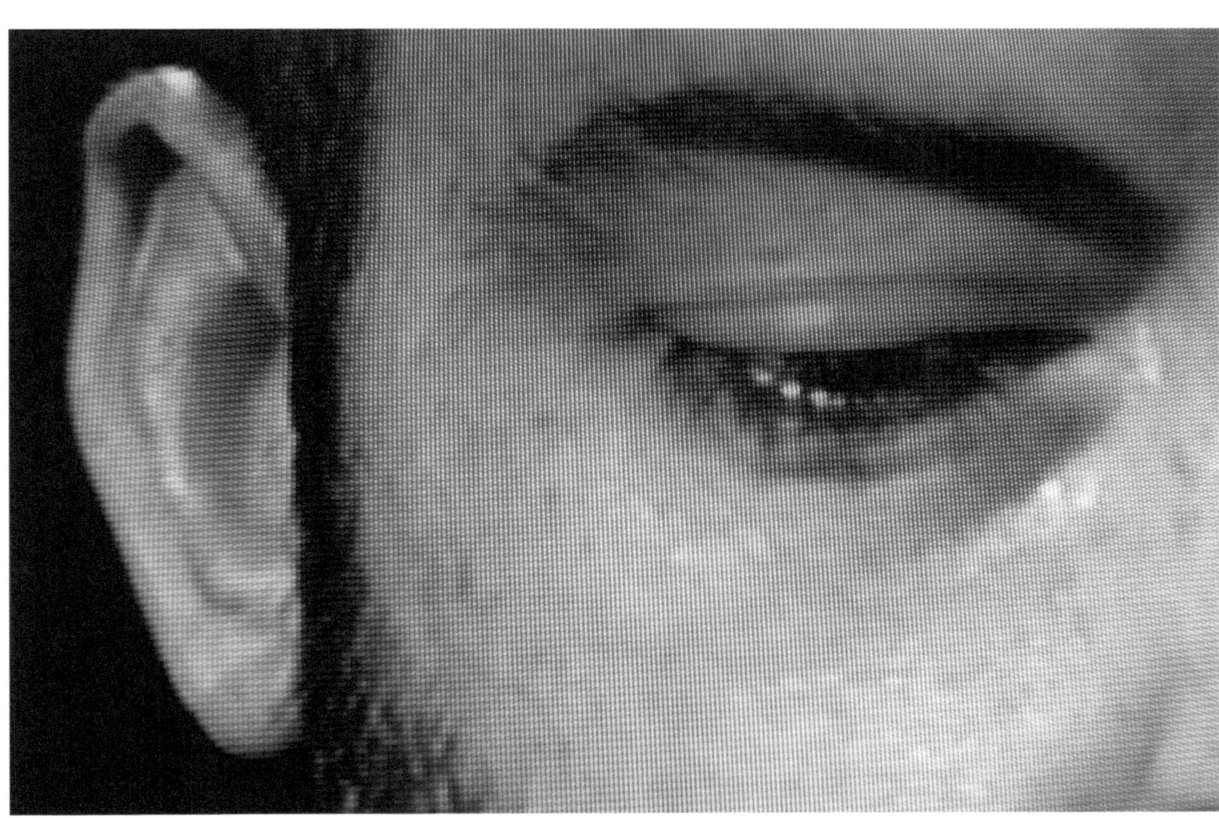

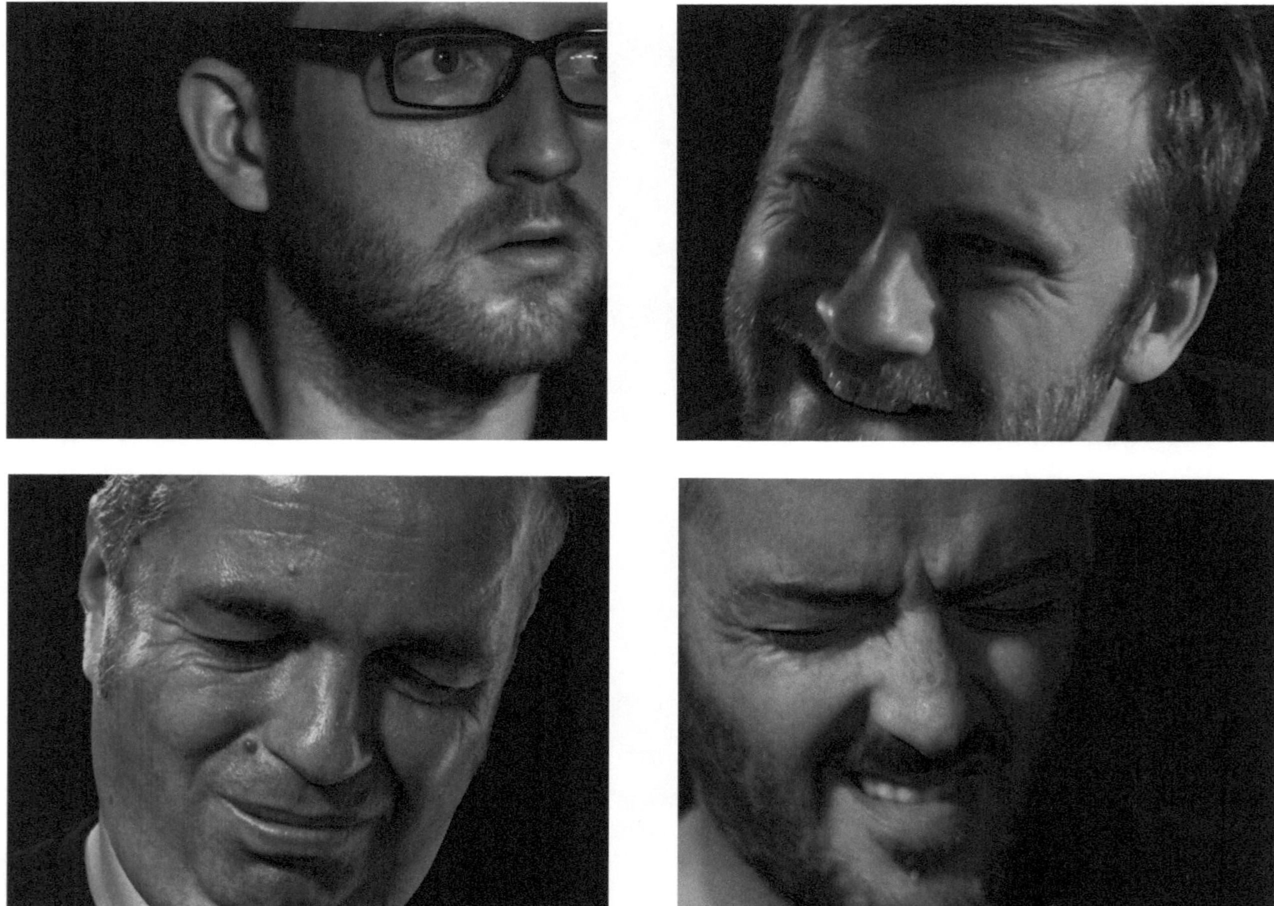

The improvisatory elements of the music are wholly reliant on an unspoken empathy between its makers. Musical gestures and phrases, their beginnings and conclusions, and their relative placements within the timeline are contingent on near extra-sensory perceptions of the individual musicians.

The Artist in Conversation with Rory MacLean

PAUL HOLMES: So just tell me your first impressions on seeing the footage. What did you think… in terms of its potential… in terms of revealing something about what the musicians are doing creatively, how do you think that's going to work?

RORY MACLEAN: I'm not sure whether we will ever be able fully to understand what's going on creatively. But what I'm interested in looking at is the interaction between musicians, and the kind of give and take, and the influence of emotions when they're playing. And to try to understand when they are experiencing this feeling of 'flow', when they're completely caught up in the moment. Hopefully we can discover that through looking at the facial expressions. Looking at it, it's quite obvious when there are moments when they're really 'in the moment'.

With other types of music, usually somebody's locked away spending a lot of time composing a piece of music, writing it down, and then it is performed at a later point. So the creative process and the creative product are separated. But in jazz improvisation, you're seeing the creative process and the creative product at the same time. You can see the individual creative process and also the group creative process. It's very much a collaborative process. And that's really interesting too.

PH: It's interesting because the artwork deliberately decontextualizes the performers from the music and the instruments and it's only about the faces. When you look at the faces they could be doing almost anything. But it seems to me when I watch it that there are very specific kinds of expressions that they seem to be making. How do you feel that they fit into work that's been done in terms of categorizing human facial expressions?

RM: This began with the work of psychologist Paul Ekman. Decades ago he devised six basic categories of emotion that could be expressed by a human face: happiness, sadness, fear, anger, surprise, and disgust.[1] And these facial expressions would be recognized in cultures throughout the world. This system is still cited in a good deal of the work that's being done around faces and emotion today.

Ekman subsequently added subtler categories to his classification, such as amusement, contentment, embarrassment, excitement, guilt, pride in achievement, relief, satisfaction, sensory pleasure, and shame.[2] I think some of those more subtle expressions might apply more to what we see here.

PH: Given the complexity of what these guys are doing facially, it strikes me that there are key moments when the expressions become very strong and pronounced. And it seems that those are the moments where we'll focus our attention. You could grab a freeze frame of that image, or perhaps a short moving-image clip, and then attempt to categorize these expressions in the way you've described.

What do people think is the function of this gurning and grimacing that the musicians appear to be doing when they're playing?

RM: It might just be the musicians' own emotional reaction to the music that they're playing. Sometimes, by moving their face, musicians can enhance their emotional expression and that can enhance their playing. But facial expressions are important to the audience too. They give the audience clues about what's happening in the music and can enhance the audience's appreciation of it, if the facial expression is showing an emotion that is congruent with it.

PH: That's quite a fascinating insight into the whole nature of performance. It suggests to me that music is not just an aural medium but a visual medium too and that the modern equivalent – MTV, the pop promo video – is not really a modern phenomenon at all but a modern manifestation of the need people have to receive visual cues to help them appreciate music. And that these grimaces evolved as an involuntary, unwitting, and therefore truthful emotional evocation of something that's actually perhaps rather abstract.

RM: Yes, even when people are listening to music without visual representation there's always imagination. I would say that it's not a pure aural experience; there's always some kind of visual component to it. Bill Thompson conducted research in Australia looking at the coupling and uncoupling of facial expressions with music.[3]

He would show the faces of musicians, for instance, who were singing unresolved, discordant music, and couple it with harmonic and melodic music. He found that these facial expressions would influence, even distort, the way the audience appreciated that music.

PH: So we should be able to do something similar with this project. We've got a soundtrack, obviously… We could play the soundtrack to non-expert members of the public, a large sample of people, and ask them to rate the music out of ten, is it as simple as that?

RM: We could have a couple of controls: one with the original facial expressions, one with neutral or deadpan expressions, and one that is emotional but has the 'wrong' emotions. We could look at the whole piece or we could look at segments.

We could ask the audience about the emotions they feel, about the level of enjoyment they feel. And so on.

PH: There'll be key milestones within the footage for each performer, won't there? Where the facial expressions are strongest. Those will be the moments where we'll want to look at the structure of what they're playing. What do you think that's going to reveal?

RM: Jane Davidson did work that looked at the way musicians look and face each other during a performance.[4] She found that there is far more eye contact at key moments such as the beginning of a piece, when there's a transition, and at the end. I think it will be interesting to examine moments when one soloist hands over to another. I would expect that there would be more non-verbal communication at those moments.

Jane Davidson's work revolved around classical music where the focus is on playing as accurately as possible. Obviously they can change the expression of the music and the tempo and so on, but the key for them is they must play the notes as written… whereas with jazz, it's much, much freer. It would be interesting to see if they need to rely on each other more, because of that freedom.

PH: This raw footage we've shot, this data if you like, it's the result of a process in which the needs of the research, and the musicians, and the artwork are all pulling in different directions.

RM: A lot of work in psychology is experimental, lab-based. But something like jazz, it's a social process; you're looking at people interacting, producing something for an audience, and you couldn't replicate that in a lab environment.

PH: It was interesting to hear from the musicians. They didn't expect it to be so obtrusive. I knew it would be obtrusive because I'd done a lot of work with musicians on TV. But they didn't realize until we stuck the cameras right in front of their faces how difficult it was going to be for them to concentrate, how hard it was for them to make eye contact with each other, and so on. It did disrupt their flow a little bit, our being there.

And from the point of view of the research, the needs of the artwork compromise the gathering of the data. I mean, for a start it's a rehearsal, not a performance. You could potentially mount miniature cameras in convenient positions very close to the musicians at a concert. They wouldn't be much more obtrusive than a stand up microphone. I think that represents a way forward for future iterations of the research. But it is an ugly aesthetic and wouldn't have worked for this artwork. In the video piece, the shots themselves had to be very well lit and composed. The idea was to achieve a level of intimacy with the subject in which you forget that there is anything around them, forget that there is anything but the face.

Notes

[1] e.g. Ekman & Friesen, 1971; Ekman & Oster, 1979.

[2] Ekman, 1999.

[3] e.g. Thompson, Graham, & Russo, 2005; Thompson & Russo, 2007; Thompson, Russo, & Livingstone, 2010.

[4] Davidson, 2012; Davidson & Good, 2002.

Bibliography

Davidson, J. W. (2012), "Bodily Movement and Facial Actions in Expressive Musical Performance by Solo and Duo Instrumentalists," *Psychology of Music* 40, 595-633.

Davidson, J. W., & Good, J. M. M. (2002), "Social and Musical Co-ordination Between Members of a String Quartet: An Exploratory Study," *Psychology of Music* 30, 186-201.

Ekman, Paul (1999), "Basic Emotions", in Dalgleish, T; Power, M, *Handbook of Cognition and Emotion*, (Chichester: John Wiley & Sons), 45-60.

Ekman, P., & Friesen, W. V. (1971), "Constants Across Cultures in the Face and Emotion," *Journal of Personality and Social Psychology* 17(2), 124-129.

Ekman, P., & Oster, H. (1979), "Facial Expressions of Emotion," *Annual Review of Psychology* 30, 527-554.

Thompson, W. F., Graham, P., & Russo, F. A. (2005), "Seeing Music Performance: Visual Influences on Perception and Experience," *Semiotica* 156, 203-227.

Thompson, W. F., & Russo, F. A. (2007), "Facing the Music," *Psychological Science* 18, 756-757.

Thompson, W. F., Russo, F. A., & Livingstone, S. L. (2010), "Facial Expressions of Singers Influence Perceived Pitch Relations," *Psychonomic Bulletin and Review* 17, 317-322.

The face unconsciously interprets
and second-guesses what is, or
will be being played. Grimace,
smile, look of surprise, of
concentrated introspection, form
a physical manifestation of
the musician's inner creative
narrative.

Biographies

Louise S. Milne is a writer and film-maker, whose research concerns the representation of dreams and nightmares. She teaches film and visual anthropology at Edinburgh College of Art and Edinburgh Napier University.

Alkistis Terzi is an award winning photographer, currently working as a freelance cinematographer and tutor in cinematography at Screen Academy Scotland.

Rory MacLean is a lecturer in Psychology at Edinburgh Napier University. His main area of research interest is creativity and its underlying cognitive processes, and he has co-authored a textbook on psychological research methods and statistics.

Haftor Medbøe is Jazz Musician in Residence and Lecturer in Composition at Edinburgh Napier University. He has recorded six albums and performs internationally with his eponymous band.

Paul Holmes spent two decades as a director in film and television before redirecting his practice towards visual art. He works in film, video and other audio-visual media.

Published in 2015 by Mutus Liber
BM Mutus Liber
London WC1N 3XX

Outside the Box © 2015 Paul Holmes

On the Rhetoric of the Face: *Outside the Box*, by Paul Holmes © 2015
Louise S. Milne

Installation photography © 2015 Alkistis Terzi

The artist in conversation © 2015 Paul Holmes and Rory MacLean

Additional text © 2015 Haftor Medbøe

Book design: Sean Martin

A CIP catalogue record for this book is available from the British Library.

ISBN-13: 978-1-908097-12-5

www.mutusliber.com